MW01268157

SLEEP
AND DREAMS

Compiled by Vijay from the writings of
Sri Aurobindo and the Mother

Sri Aurobindo Society

AUROPUBLICATIONS

POWERFUL THOUGHTS, INSPIRING VISION

Yoga in Everyday Life – Booklet Series

ISBN 978-81-7060-097-8

First Centenary Edition: 1972
Fourth Revised Edition: 1995
Ninth Reprint: 2016

Published by
AuroPublications, Sri Aurobindo Society, Puducherry
Website: www.auropublications.org | www.aurosociety.org
Email: info@auropublications.org
Printed at Sri Aurobindo Ashram Press, Puducherry, India

This is one in a series of thirty booklets published by the Sri Aurobindo Society under the title "Yoga in Everyday Life." Our effort is to bring together, from Sri Aurobindo and the Mother, simple passages with a practical orientation on specific subjects, so that everyone may feel free to choose a book according to his inner need. The topics cover the whole field of human activity, because true spirituality is not the rejection of life but the art of perfecting life.

While the passages from Sri Aurobindo are in the original English, most of the passages from the Mother (selections from her talks and writings) are translations from the original French. We must also bear in mind that the excerpts have been taken out of their original context and that a compilation, in its very nature, is likely to have a personal and subjective approach. A sincere attempt, however, has been made to be faithful to the vision of Sri Aurobindo and the Mother.

We hope these booklets will inspire the readers to go to the complete works and will help them to mould their lives and their enviornments towards an ever greater perfection. The quotations from Sri Aurobindo are prefaced by his symbol and those from the Mother by her symbol.

The Mother's   Sri Aurobindo's

"O TRUTH, COME, MANIFEST."

"आयाहि सत्य आविर्भव"

CONTENTS

THE NECESSITY OF SLEEP

...Sleep is necessary for the body just as food is. Sufficient sleep must be taken, but no excessive sleep. What sufficient sleep is depends on the need of the body.

*

It is a great mistake not to take sufficient sleep. Seven hours is the minimum needed. When one has a very strong nervous system one can reduce it to six, sometimes even five – but it is rare and ought not to be attempted without necessity.

*

Both for fevers and for mental trouble sleep is a great help and its absence very undesirable – it is the loss of a curative agency.

*

It is not a right method to try to keep awake at night; the suppression of the needed sleep makes the body tamasic and unfit for the necessary concentration during the waking hours. The right way is to transform the sleep and not suppress it, and especially to learn how to become more and more conscious in sleep itself. If that is done, sleep changes into an inner mode of consciousness in which the sadhana can continue as much as in the waking state, and at the same time one is able to enter into other planes of consciousness than the physical and command an immense range of informative and utilisable experience.

*

To begin with, we should remember that more than one third of our existence is spent in sleeping and that, consequently, the time devoted to physical sleep well deserves our attention.

I say physical sleep, for it would be wrong to think that our whole being sleeps when our bodies are asleep.

HOW TO SLEEP

How is it better to go to bed early and to get up early?

When the sun sets, a kind of peace descends upon the earth and this peace is helpful for sleep.

When the sun rises, a vigorous energy descends upon the earth and this energy is helpful for work.

When you go to bed late and get up late, you contradict the forces of Nature and that is not very wise.

*

Why are the hours before midnight better for sleep than the later hours?

Because, symbolically, during the hours till midnight, the sun is setting, while from the very first hour after midnight the sun begins to rise.

*

The quality of sleep is much more important than its quantity. In order to have a truly effective rest and relaxation during sleep, it is good as a rule to drink something before going to bed, a cup of milk or soup or fruit-juice, for instance. Light food brings a quiet sleep. One should, however, abstain from all copious meals, for then the sleep becomes agitated and is disturbed by nightmares, or else is dense, heavy and dulling. But the most important thing of all is to make the mind clear, to quieten the emotions and calm the effervescence of desires and the preoccupations which accompany them. If before retiring to bed one has talked a lot or had a lively discussion, if one has read an exciting or intensely interesting book, one should rest a little without sleeping in order to quieten the mental activity, so that the brain does not engage in disorderly movements while the other parts of the body alone are asleep. Those who practise meditation will do well to concentrate for a few minutes on a lofty and restful idea, in an aspiration towards a higher and vaster consciousness. Their sleep will benefit greatly from this and they will largely be spared the risk of falling into unconsciousness while they sleep.

*

To sleep well one must learn how to sleep.

If one is physically very tired, it is better not to go to sleep immediately, otherwise one falls into the inconscient. If one is very tired, one must stretch out on the bed, relax, loosen all the nerves one after another until one becomes like a rumpled cloth in one's bed, as though one had neither bones nor muscles. When one has done that, the same thing must be done in the mind. Relax, do not concentrate on any idea or try to solve a problem or ruminate on impressions, sensations or emotions you had during the day. All that must be allowed to drop off quietly: one gives oneself up, one is indeed like a rag. When you have succeeded in doing this, there is always a little flame, there – that flame never goes out and you become conscious of it when you have managed this relaxation. And all of a sudden this little flame rises slowly into an aspiration for the

3

divine life, the truth, the consciousness of the Divine, the union with the inner being, it goes higher and higher, it rises, rises, like that, very gently. Then everything gathers there, and if at that moment you fall asleep, you have the best sleep you could possibly have. I guarantee that if you do this carefully, you are sure to sleep, and also sure that instead of falling into a dark hole you will sleep in light, and when you get up in the morning you will be fresh, fit, content, happy and full of energy for the day.

*

 Even for those who have never been in trance, it is good to repeat a mantra, a word, a prayer before going into sleep. But there must be a life in the words; I do not mean an intellectual significance, nothing of that kind, but a vibration. And its effect on the body is extraordinary: it begins to vibrate, vibrate, vibrate... and quietly you let yourself go, as though you wanted to go to sleep. The body vibrates more and more, more and more, more and more, and away you go. That is the cure for tamas.

It is tamas which causes bad sleep. There are two kinds of bad sleep: the sleep that makes you heavy, dull, as if you lost all the effect of the effort you put in during the preceding day; and the sleep that exhausts you as if you had passed your time in fighting. I have noticed that if you cut your sleep into slices (it is a habit one can form), the nights become better. That is to say, you must be able to come back to your normal consciousness and normal aspiration at fixed intervals – come back at the call of the consciousness. But for that you must not use an alarm-clock! When you are in trance, it is not good to be shaken out of it.

When you are about to go to sleep, you can make a formation;

say: "I shall wake up at such an hour" (you do that very well when you are a child). For the first stretch of sleep you must count at least three hours; for the last, one hour is sufficient. But the first one must be three hours at the minimum. On the whole, you have to remain in bed at least seven hours; in six hours you do not have time enough to do much (naturally I am looking at it from the point of view of sadhana) to make the nights useful.

To make use of the nights is an excellent thing. It has a double effect: a negative effect, it prevents you from falling backward, losing what you have gained – that is indeed painful – and a positive effect, you make some progress, you continue your progress. You make use of the night, so there is no trace of fatigue any more.

Two things you must eliminate: falling into the stupor of the inconscience, with all the things of the subconscient and inconscient that rise up, invade you, enter you; and a vital and mental superactivity where you pass your time in fighting, literally, terrible battles. People come out of that state bruised, as if they had received blows. And they did receive them – it is not "as if"! And I see only one way out: to change the nature of sleep.

WHAT HAPPENS DURING SLEEP

According to a recent medical theory one passes in sleep through many phases until one arrives at a state in which there is absolute rest and silence – it lasts only for ten minutes, the rest of the time is taken up by travelling to that and travelling back again to the waking state. I suppose the ten minutes sleep can be called *suśupti* in the Brahman or Brahmaloka, the rest is *svapna* or passage through other worlds (planes or states of conscious existence). It is these ten minutes that restore the energies of

5

the being, and without it sleep is not refreshing.

According to the Mother's experience and knowledge one passes from waking through a succession of states of sleep consciousness which are in fact an entry and passage into so many worlds and arrives at a pure Sachchidananda state of complete rest, light and silence, – afterwards one retraces one's way till one reaches the waking physical state. It is this Sachchidananda period that gives sleep all its restorative value. These two accounts, the scientific and the occult-spiritual, are practically identical with each other. But the former is only a recent discovery of what the occult-spiritual knowledge knew long ago.

People's ideas of sound sleep are absolutely erroneous. What they call sound sleep is merely a plunge of the outer consciousness into a complete subconscience. They call that a dreamless sleep; but it is only a state in which the surface sleep consciousness which is a subtle prolongation of the outer still left active in sleep itself is unable to record the dreams and transmit them to the physical mind. As a matter of fact the whole sleep is full of dreams. It is only during the brief time in which one is in the Brahmaloka that the dreams cease.

*

 The rule should be to call the Mother before sleeping, to concentrate on her and try to feel the Mother's protection around her and go with that into sleep. In the dream itself a habit of calling the Mother when in difficulty or peril should be formed; many sadhaks do it. Not to allow the invasion, any invasion of any power or being, whether in dream, meditation or otherwise – no force except the Divine Force, means to reject it, never to give assent, whether through attention or through weakness....

DREAMS – NATURE AND IMPORTANCE

 In principle, to judge the activities of sleep one needs the same capacity of discrimination as to judge the waking activities.

But since we usually give the name "dream" to a considerable number of activities that differ completely from one another, the first point is to learn to distinguish between these various activities – that is, to recognise what part of the being it is that "dreams", what domain it is that one "dreams" and what the nature of that activity is. In his letters, Sri Aurobindo has given very complete and detailed descriptions and explanations of all the activities of sleep. Reading these letters is a good introduction to the study of this subject and to its practical application.

*

 The doctors who carried out these experiments were led to the conclusion that mental activity never really ceases; and it is this activity which is more or less confusedly transcribed in our brains by what we know as dreams. Thus, whether we are aware of it or not, we always dream.

Certainly, it is possible to suppress this activity completely and to have a total, dreamless sleep; but to be able in this way to immerse our mental being in a repose similar to the repose of our physical being, we must have achieved a perfect control over it, and this is not an easy thing to do.

In most cases, this activity is even heightened, because, as the body is asleep, the internal faculties are no longer focussed on or used by the physical life.

*

It is sometimes said that in a man's sleep his true nature is revealed.

Indeed, it often happens that the sensory being, which throughout the whole day has been subjected to the control of the active will, reacts all the more violently during the night when this constraint is no longer effective.

All the desires that have been repressed without being dissolved – and this dissociation can only be obtained after much sound and wide-ranging analysis – seek satisfaction while the will is dormant.

And since desires are true dynamic centres of formation, they tend to organise, within and around us, the combination of circumstances that is most favourable to their satisfaction.

In this way the fruit of many efforts made by our conscious thought during the day can be destroyed in a few hours at night.

This is one of the main causes of the resistances which our will for progress often encounters within us, of the difficulties which sometimes appear insurmountable to us and which we are unable to explain, because our goodwill seems so integral to us.

We must therefore learn to know our dreams, and first of all to distinguish between them, for they are very varied in nature and quality. In the course of one night we may often have several dreams which belong to different categories, depending on the depth of our sleep.

*

As a general rule, each individual has a period of the night that is more favourable for dreams, during which his activity is more fertile, more intellectual, and the mental circumstances of the environment in which he moves are more interesting.

*

 If one eats a heavy meal, why is the sleep disturbed by nightmares?

Because there is a very close connection between dreams and the condition of the stomach. Observations have been made and it has been noticed that in accordance with what is eaten, dreams are of one kind or another, and that if the digestion is difficult, the dream always turns into a nightmare – those nightmares which have no reality but still are nightmares all the same and very unpleasant – seeing tigers, cats, etc... or else you experience things like... for instance, you are facing a great danger and must hurry up, get dressed quickly and go out, and then you can't dress, try as you will, you can't put on your things, you don't find your things any more, and if you want to put on your shoes they never fit you, and if you want to go somewhere very fast, the legs don't move any longer, they are paralysed and you are stuck there making formidable efforts to advance, and you can't move. It is this kind of nightmare that comes from a disordered stomach.

*

The great majority of dreams have no other value than that of a purely mechanical and uncontrolled activity of the physical brain, in which certain cells continue to function during sleep as generators of sensory images and impressions conforming to the pictures received from outside.

9

These dreams are nearly always caused by purely physical circumstances – state of health, digestion, position in bed, etc.

With a little self-observation and a few precautions, it is easy to avoid this type of dream, which is as useless as it is tiring, by eliminating its physical causes.

There are also other dreams which are nothing but futile manifestations of the erratic activities of certain mental faculties, which associate ideas, conversations and memories that come together at random.

Such dreams are already more significant, for these erratic activities reveal to us the confusion that prevails in our mental being as soon as it is no longer subject to the control of our will, and show us that this being is still not organised or ordered within us, that it is not mature enough to have an autonomous life.

Almost the same in form to these, but more important in their consequences, are the dreams which I mentioned just now, those which arise from the inner being seeking revenge when it is freed for a moment from the constraint that we impose upon it. These dreams often enable us to perceive tendencies, inclinations, impulses, desires of which we were not conscious so long as our will to realise our ideal kept them concealed in some obscure recess of our being.

*

 You will easily understand that rather than letting them live on unknown to us, it is better to bring them boldly and courageously to the light, so as to force them to leave us for ever.

We should therefore observe our dreams attentively; they are often useful instructors who can give us a powerful help on our way towards self-conquest.

No one knows himself well who does not know the unconfined activities of his nights, and no man can call himself his own master unless he has the perfect consciousness and mastery of the numerous actions he performs during his physical sleep.

REMEMBERING DREAMS

 Why do we forget our dreams?

Because you do not dream always at the same place. It is not always the same part of your being that dreams and it is not at the same place that you dream. If you were in conscious, direct, continuous communication with all the parts of your being, you would remember all your dreams. But very few parts of the being are in communication.

For example, you have a dream in the subtle physical, that is to say, quite close to the physical. Generally, these dreams occur in the early hours of the morning, that is between four and five o'clock, at the end of the sleep. If you do not make a sudden movement when you wake up, if you remain very quiet, very still and a little attentive – quietly attentive – and concentrated, you will remember them, for the communication between the subtle physical and the physical is established – very rarely is there no communication.

Now, dreams are mostly forgotten because you have a dream while in a certain state and then pass into another. For instance, when you sleep, your body is asleep, your vital is asleep, but your mind is still active. So your mind begins to have dreams,

11

that is, its activity is more or less coordinated, the imagination is very active and you see all kinds of things, take part in extraordinary happenings.... After some time, all that calms down and the mind also begins to doze. The vital that was resting wakes up; it comes out of the body, walks about, goes here and there, does all kinds of things, reacts, sometimes fights, and finally eats. It does all kinds of things. The vital is very adventurous. It watches. When it is heroic it rushes to save people who are in prison or to destroy enemies or it makes wonderful discoveries. But this pushes back the whole mental dream very far behind. It is rubbed off, forgotten: naturally you cannot remember it because the vital dream takes its place. But if you wake up suddenly at that moment, you remember it. There are people who have made the experiment, who have got up at certain fixed hours of the night and when they wake up suddenly, they do remember. You must not move brusquely, but awake in the natural course, then you remember.

After a time, the vital having taken a good stroll, needs to rest also, and so it goes into repose and quietness, quite tired at the end of all kinds of adventures. Then something else wakes up. Let us suppose that it is the subtle physical that goes for a walk. It starts moving and begins wandering, seeing the rooms and... why, this thing that was there, but it has come here and that other thing which was in that room is now in this one, and so on. If you wake up without stirring, you remember. But this has pushed away far to the back of the consciousness all the stories of the vital. They are forgotten and so you cannot recollect your dreams. But if at the time of waking up you are not in a hurry, you are not obliged to leave your bed, on the contrary you can remain there as long as you wish, you need not even open your eyes; you keep your head exactly where it was and you make yourself like a tranquil mirror within and concentrate there. You catch just a tiny end of the tail of your dream. You catch it and start pulling gently, without stirring in the least. You begin pulling quite gently, and then first one part comes, a little later another. You go backward; the last comes up first. Everything goes backward, slowly, and suddenly the whole dream reappears: "Ah, there! it was like that." Above all, do not jump up, do not stir; you repeat the dream to yourself several times – once, twice – until it becomes clear in all its details. Once that dream is settled, you continue not to stir, you try to go further in, and suddenly you catch the tail of something else. It is more distant, more vague, but you can still seize it. And here also you hang on, get hold of it and pull, and you see that everything changes and you enter another world; all of a sudden you have an extraordinary adventure – it is another dream. You follow the same process. You repeat the dream to yourself once, twice, until you are sure of it. You remain very quiet all the time. Then you begin to penetrate still more deeply into yourself, as though you were going in very far, very far; and again suddenly you see a vague form, you have a feeling, a sensation... like a current of air, a slight breeze, a little breath; and you say, "Well, well...." It takes a form, it becomes clear – and the third category comes. You must have a lot of time, a lot of patience, you must be very quiet in your mind and body, very quiet, and you can tell the story of your whole night from the end right up to the beginning.

Even without doing this exercise which is very long and difficult, in order to recollect a dream, whether it be the last one or the one in the middle that has made a violent impression on your being, you must do what I have said when you wake up: take particular care not even to move your head on the pillow, remain absolutely still and let the dream return.

Some people do not have a passage between one state and another, there is a little gap and so they leap from one to the other; there is no highway passing through all the states of being with no break of the consciousness. A small dark hole, and you do not remember. It is like a precipice across which one has to extend the consciousness. To build a bridge takes a very long time; it takes much longer than building a physical bridge.... Very few people want to and know how to do it. They may have had magnificent activities, they do not remember them or sometimes only the last, the nearest, the most physical activity, with an uncoordinated movement – dreams having no sense.

But there are as many different kinds of nights and sleep as there are different days and activities. There are not many days that are alike, each day is different. The days are not the same, the nights are not the same. You and your friends are doing apparently the same thing, but for each one it is very different. And each one must have his own procedure.

*

 Is it useful to note down one's dreams?

Yes, for more than a year I applied myself to this kind of self-discipline. I noted down everything – a few words, just a little thing, an impression – and I tried to pass from one memory to another. At first it was not very fruitful, but at the end of about fourteen months I could follow, beginning from the end, all the movements, all the dreams right up to the beginning of the night.

*

 When we sleep, our consciousness goes out, doesn't it? But other people have dreams in which I appear. So what happens? Does the consciousness divide itself or are other people's dreams only their own imagination?

Most often, it is the vital consciousness that goes out of the body and has the form, the appearance of the person's body. If one person dreams of another, it means that both have met at night, most often in the vital region, but it can also happen elsewhere, in the subtle physical or the mental. There are any number of different possibilities in dreams.

CONTROL OVER DREAMS

 When you are very tired and in need of rest and if you know how to exteriorise yourself, if you go out of your body and enter consciously into the vital world, there are regions there, in the vital world, which are like a marvellous virgin forest, with all the splendour of a rich and harmonious vegetation, and beautiful, mirror – like pools. And the atmosphere is filled with the living vitality of plants, with every shade of green reflected in the water... And there you feel so much life, so much beauty, so much richness and plenitude that you wake up full of energy. And all this is so objective! I have been able to take people there, without telling them anything at all about how it would be, and they were able to describe the place exactly as I can myself, and they had exactly the same experience. They were absolutely exhausted before going to sleep and they woke up with an absolutely marvellous feeling of plenitude, of force and energy. They had stayed there only a few minutes.

There are regions like that – not many, but they exist. On the other hand, there are many unpleasant places in the vital world and it is better not to go there. Leaving aside those who are so attached, so rivetted to their bodies that they don't even want to leave them, those who can easily learn to go out of their bodies ought to do so with great care. I haven't been able to teach this to many people, for that would mean exposing them, sometimes

15

without protection – when they do it alone, without my presence – to experiences which can be extremely harmfull to them.

The Vital world is a world of extremes. If, for example, you eat a bunch of grapes in the vital world, you can go for thirtysix hours without feeling hungry – fully nourished. But you can meet with certain things, enter certain places that drain all your energy in a trice, and sometimes leave you with illnesses and after-effects that belong to the vital world....

*

 You have said that one can exercise one's conscious will and change the course of one's dreams.

Ah, Yes, I have already told you that once. If you are in the middle of a dream and something happens which you don't like (for instance, somebody shouts that he wants to kill you), you say: "That won't do at all, I don't want my dream to be like that", and you can change the action or the ending. You can organise your dream as you want. One can arrange one's dreams. But for this you must be conscious that you are dreaming, you must know you are dreaming.

*

 Every evening when they (some children) go to bed they return to the same place and continue their dream....

Nothing is more interesting. It is a most pleasant way of passing the nights. You begin a story, then, when it is time to wake up, you put a full stop to the last sentence and come back into your body. And then the following night you start off again, re-open the page and resume your story during the whole time you are out; and then you arrange things well – they must be well arranged, it must be very beautiful. And when it is time to come back, you put a full stop once again and tell those things, "Stay very quiet till I return!" And you come back into your body. And you continue this every evening and write a book of wonderful fairy-tales – provided you remember them when you wake up.

But this depends on being in a quiet state during the day, doesn't it?

No, it depends on the candour of the child.

And on the trust he has in what happens to him, on the absence of the mind's critical sense, and a simplicity of heart, and a youthful and active energy – it depends on all that – on a kind of inner vital generosity: one must not be too egoistic, one must not be too miserly, nor too practical, too utilitarian – indeed there are all sorts of things one should not be... like children. And then, one must have a lively power of imagination, for – I seem to be telling you stupid things, but it is quite true – there is a world in which you are the supreme maker of forms: that is your own particular vital world. You are the supreme fashioner and you can make a marvel of your world if you know how to use it. If you have an artistic or poetic consciousness, if you love harmony, beauty, you will build there something marvellous which will tend to spring up into the material manifestation.

When I was small I used to call this "telling stories to oneself". It is not at all a telling with words, in one's head: it is a going away to this place which is fresh and pure, and... building up a wonderful story there. And if you know how to tell yourself a story in this way, and if it is truly beautiful, truly harmonious, truly powerful and well co-ordinated, this story will be realised in your life – perhaps not exactly in the form in which you created it, but as a more or less changed physical expression of what you made.

That may take years, perhaps, but your story will tend to organise your life.

But there are very few people who know how to tell a beautiful story; and then they always mix horrors in it, which they regret later.

If one could create a magnificent story without any horror in it, nothing but beauty, it would have a *considerable* influence on everyone's life. And this is what people don't know.

If one knew how to use this power, this creative power in the world of vital forms, if one knew how to use this while yet a child, a very small child... for it is then that one fashions his material destiny. But usually people around you, sometimes even your own little friends, but mostly parents and teachers, dabble in it and spoil everything for you, so well that very seldom does the thing succeed completely.

But otherwise, if it were done like that, with the spontaneous candour of a child, you could organise a wonderful life for yourself — I am speaking of the physical world.

The dreams of childhood are the realities of mature age.

DREAMS AND THEIR INTERPRETATIONS

 But dreams are not merely the malignant informers of our weaknesses or the malicious destroyers of our daily effort for progress.

Although there are dreams which we should contend with or transform, there are others which should on the contrary be cultivated as precious auxiliaries in our work within and around us.

There can be no doubt that from many points of view our subconscient knows more than our habitual consciousness.

Who has not had the experience of metaphysical, moral or practical problem with which we grapple in vain in the evening, and whose solution, impossible to find then, appears clearly and accurately in the morning on waking?

The mental enquiry had been going on throughout the period of sleep and the internal faculties, freed from all material activity, were able to concentrate solely on the subject of their interest.

Very often, the work itself remains unconscious; only the result is perceived....

*

Recently, a writer was preoccupied with a half-written chapter which he was unable to finish.

His mind, particularly interested in this work of composition, continued the chapter during the night, and the more it phrased and rephrased the ideas making up the various paragraphs, it became aware that these ideas were not expressed in the most rational order and that the paragraphs had to be rearranged.

All this work was transcribed in the consciousness of our writer in the following dream: he was in his study with several armchairs which he had just brought there and was arranging and rearranging them in the room, until he found the most suitable place for each one.

In the knowledge that certain people may have had of such inadequate transcriptions, we can find the origin of the popular beliefs, the "dream-books" which are the delight of so many simple souls.

But it is easy to understand that this clumsy transcription has a particular form for each individual; each one makes his own distortion.

Consequently, an excessive generalisation of certain interpretations which may have been quite correct for the person applying them to his own case, merely gives rise to vulgar and foolish superstitions.

*

 On the mental plane all the formations made by the mind – the actual "forms" that it gives to the thoughts – return and appear to you as if they were coming from outside and give you dreams. Most dreams are like that. Some people have a very conscious mental life and are able to enter the mental plane and move about in it with the same independence they have in physical life; these people have mentally objective nights. But most people are incapable of doing this: it is their mental activity going on during sleep and assuming forms, and these forms give them what they call dreams.

There is a very common example – it is amusing because it is rather vivid. If you have quarrelled with someone during the day, you may wish to hit him, to say very unpleasant things to him. You control yourself, you don't do it, but your thought, your mind is at work and in your sleep you suddenly have a terrible dream. Someone approaches you with a stick and you hit each other and have a real fight. And when you wake up, if you don't know, if you don't understand what has happened, you say to yourself, "What an unpleasant dream I had!" But in fact it is your own thought which came back to you, like that. So be on your guard when you dream that someone is unkind to you! First of all, you should ask yourself, "But didn't I have a bad thought against him?".

*

 The cerebral transcription of the activities of the night is sometimes warped to such an extent that phenomena are perceived as the opposite of what they really are.

For example, when you have a bad thought against someone and when this bad thought, left to itself, gathers full force during the night, you dream that the person in question is beating you, is doing you some bad turn, or even wounding you or trying to kill you.

Moreover, as a general rule, we should take great intellectual precautions before interpreting a dream, and above all, we should review exhaustively all the subjective explanations before we assign to it the value of an objective reality.

However, especially in those who have unlearnt the habit of always directing their thoughts towards themselves, there are cases where we can observe events outside ourselves, events which are not the reflection of our personal mental constructions. And if we know how to translate into intellectual language the more or less inadequate images into which the brain has translated these events, we can learn many things that our too limited physical faculties do not allow us to perceive.

PREMONITORY DREAMS

There are all kinds of premonitory dreams. There are premonitory dreams that are fulfilled immediately, that is to say, you dream in the night what will happen on the next day, and there are premonitory dreams that are fulfilled over varying lengths of time. And according to their position in time, these dreams are seen on various planes.

The higher we rise towards absolute certainty, the greater the distance is, because these visions belong to a region which is very close to the Origin and the length of time between the revelation of what is going to be and its realisation may be very great. But the revelation is certain, because it is very close to the Origin. There is a place – when one is identified with the Supreme – where one knows everything absolutely, in the past, the present, the future and everywhere. But usually people who go there forget what they have seen when they return. An extremely strict discipline is needed to remember. And that is the only place where one cannot make a mistake....

*

When events are already prepared in the subtle physical and you have a vision of them, is it too late to change things? Can one still act?

I know of a very interesting example. There was a time when in the newspaper "Le Matin" – it was a long time ago, you must have been very young – every day there was a little cartoon of a boy pointing to something – a kind of page-boy dressed like that – and always showing the date or something – a little cartoon. Now the gentleman in this story was travelling and he was staying in a big hotel, I do not remember in which town, and one night or early in the morning, very early, he had a dream. He saw this page-boy pointing to his funeral carriage – you know, when they take people to the cemetery, in Europe – and inviting him to step into it! He saw that and then in the morning when he was ready, he left his room which was on the top floor, and there, on the landing, the same boy, dressed in the same way, was pointing out the lift for him to go down. That gave him a shock. He refused and said, "No thank you." The lift fell and crashed, killing the people inside.

He told me that after that he believed in dreams.

It was a vision. He saw the boy, but instead of the lift, the boy was showing him his hearse. So when he saw the same gesture, the same boy – like the cartoon, you see – he said, "No thank you, I'll walk down", and the machine – it was one of those hydraulic lifts – broke and fell. It was right at the top. It was crushed to a pulp.

My explanation is that an entity had forewarned him. The image of the page-boy seems to indicate that an intelligence, a consciousness had intervened; it does not seem to have been his own subconscient. Or it might be that his subconscient was aware and had seen in the subtle physical that this was going to happen. But why did his subconscient give him an image like that? I do not know. Perhaps something in the subconscient knew, because it was already there, it was already in the subtle physical. The accident already existed before it happened – the law of the accident.

SOMNAMBULISM

At times when one goes out of the body, the body follows the part which goes out.

You are speaking of a somnambulist? But that is quite another thing. This means that the part which goes out (whether a part of the mind or a part of the vital) is so strongly attached to the body, or rather that the body is so attached to this part, that when this part decides to do something the body follows it automatically. In your inner being you decide to do a certain thing and your body is so closely tied to your inner being that without thinking of it, without wanting to do so, without making any effort, it follows and does the same thing. Note that in this matter, the physical body has capacities it would not have in the ordinary waking condition. For instance, it is well known that one can walk in dangerous places where one would find it rather difficult to walk in the waking state. The body follows the consciousness of the inner being and its own consciousness is asleep – for the body has a consciousness. All the parts of the being, including the most material, have an independent consciousness. Hence when you go to sleep dead tired, when your physical body needs rest absolutely, your physical consciousness sleeps, while the consciousness of your subtle physical body or your vital or of your mind does not sleep, it continues its activity; but your physical consciousness is separated from the body, it is asleep in a state of unconsciousness, and then the part which does not sleep, which is active, uses the body without the physical consciousness as intermediary and makes it do things directly. That is how one becomes a somnambulist. According to my experience, the waking consciousness goes to sleep, for some reason or other (usually due to fatigue), but the inner being is awake, and the body is so tied to it that it follows it automatically. That is why you do fantastic things, because you

24

do not see them physically, you see them in a different way.

*

How can one be cured of somnambulism?

Quite simply, by putting a will upon the body before going to sleep. One becomes a somnambulist because the mind is not developed enough to break the inner ties. For the mind always separates the external being from the deeper consciousness. Little children are quite tied up. I knew children who were quite sincere but could not distinguish whether a thing was going on in their imagination or in reality. For them the inner life was as real as the external life. They were not telling stories, they were not liars; simply the inner life was as real as the external life. There are children who go night after night to the same spot in order to continue the dream they have begun – they are experts in the art of going out of their bodies.

Is it good to leave the body asleep and go out rambling? Can one go back into the body at any moment one likes?

It is dangerous if you sleep surrounded by people who may come and shake you up, believing that something has happened to you. But if you are alone and sleep quietly, there is no danger.

One can get back into the body at any time and generally it is much more difficult to remain outside than to get back – as soon as the least thing happens, one rushes back quickly into the body.

If one goes out of the body leaving it on the bed, can someone else enter it?

25

That can happen but it is extremely rare, once in a hundred thousand cases.

"Someone" cannot enter – a human being cannot enter the body of another unless he has quite an exceptional and unique occult knowledge and in that case he will not do it.

But if a human being does not enter, at times there are beings of the vital world who do not have a body and want to have one for the fun of the experience, and when they see that someone has gone out of the body (but he must go out very materially) and is not sufficiently protected, they can rush in to take his place. But it is such a rare thing that if you had not put the question I would not have spoken about it. Still it is not an impossibility.

People who have nightmares of this kind should always protect themselves occultly before going out of the body – it can be done in many ways. The simplest way, one which needs no special knowledge is to call the Guru or, if one knows somebody who has the knowledge, to call him in thought or spirit; or to protect oneself by making a kind of wall of protection around oneself (one can do many things, can't one?); this can prevent such beings from entering.

If you have a disposition for exteriorisation and if you follow a yoga, you are always asked to protect your sleep: by some contemplation, a mental movement, any movement – there are many ways of protecting oneself. But I think there is no such danger for you; perhaps not for everybody, but still one would have to be terribly ambitious, terribly insincere for such a thing to happen; one would have to be in relation with truly wicked entities, for, a being who lives in orderliness and truth will never rush into the body of another, that is an act of disorder and it is not done.

*

At times I talk in my sleep. It is a sign that the mind lacks control, isn't it? So what should I do to keep it quiet at night?

Generally when the body is asleep at night, the mind goes out because it is difficult for it to remain quiet for a long time; and that is why most people do not talk.

But your mind seems to remain in your body, so you must ask it to remain perfectly quiet and silent so that your body can rest properly. A little concentration for that, before going to sleep, will surely be effective.

LET US CULTIVATE OUR NIGHTS

Uncultivated lands produce weeds. We do not want any weeds in ourselves, so let us cultivate the vast field of our nights.

You must not think that this can be in the least harmful to the depth of your sleep and the efficacy of a repose which is not only indispensable but beneficial. On the contrary, there are many people whose nights are more tiring than their days, for reasons which often elude them; they should become conscious of these reasons so that their will can begin to act on them and remove their effects, that is, to put a stop to these activities which in such cases are nearly always useless and even harmful.

If our night has enabled us to gain some new knowledge – the solution of a problem, a contact of our inner being with some centre of life or light, or even the accomplishment of some useful task – we shall always wake up with a feeling of strength and well-being. The hours that are wasted in doing nothing good or useful are the most tiring.

REFERENCES – SLEEP AND DREAMS

N.B. Abbreviations: SABCL – Sri Aurobindo Birth Centenary Library
MCW – Mother's Collected Works

The quotation in the last line of the introduction is from 'White Roses'.